Brief Guide for
Teaching Adult Learners

Cheryl Torok Fleming
J. Bradley Garner

TRIANGLE PUBLISHING
Marion, Indiana

Brief Guide for Teaching Adult Learners
Cheryl Torok Fleming and J. Bradley Garner

Direct correspondence and permission requests to one of the following:

E-mail: info@trianglepublishing.com
Web site: www.trianglepublishing.com
Mail: Triangle Publishing
            Indiana Wesleyan University
            1900 West 50th Street
            Marion, Indiana 46953

The *Chicago Manual of Style* is the preferred style guide of Triangle Publishing.

Copyright © 2009 by Triangle Publishing
Published by Triangle Publishing
Marion, Indiana 46953
Printed in the United States of America

ISBN: 978-1-931283-40-3

Cover design: Jim Pardew
Graphic design: Lyn Rayn

CONTENTS

PREFACE
Welcoming Adult Learners

Andragogy is the true method of adult learning . . . life itself is the adult's school.

—Martha Anderson and Eduard Lindeman

Dawn is thirty-eight years old, a high school graduate, recently divorced, and a single parent. She is employed full-time in a job that she would describe as "tolerable." Dawn views her current job merely as a way to pay the bills. Lately she has been thinking about the need to get some additional training if she is to realize her dreams of owning a home and providing a financially secure future for her children.

At a deeper level, Dawn also talks openly about wanting a career that affirms her sense of life purpose and that fully exercises her gifts and talents. In response to these feelings, she has started to investigate the various options that might be available to her as an adult learner. Her priorities include an educational program that will acknowledge her unique life experiences, appreciate the urgency of completing a course of study within a reasonable time and at a manageable cost, and accommodate the many aspects of her life that must be balanced, and sometimes juggled, as she meets the other demands of her life.

A growing population of adults finds itself in Dawn's situation, or feel a similar need for opportunities to learn and grow. These adults are seeking ways to engage with some type of learning environment or program that connects with their unique needs. They might find themselves in this situation because of corporate downsizing, or simply because they don't feel any fulfillment in their current situation.

These adults make the commitments necessary to engage in learning opportunities for their own unique reasons: to gain new skills, qualify for their dream jobs, fill an indescribable void in their lives, or pursue a future that they envision for themselves. Although their reasons for enrolling are unique, in many ways they share a common bond as adult learners. In any event, they expect learning experiences that are relevant to their needs and preferences.

HOW THIS TEXT IS ORGANIZED

Approaching the unique needs of adult learners requires that we consider the best available theories and practices. In chapter 1, we'll examine some of the best-known and most thoroughly documented theories of adult learning: Knowles' concepts and characteristics of adult learners, self-directed learning, experiential learning, learner-centered instructional practices, motivational and affective factors, and transformative learning. Each of these perspectives provides vantage points from which to understand the learner and to begin thinking about how these theories might be implemented in a classroom setting.

To address the various approaches and strategies that might be helpful in working with adult learners, we have adapted the work of Knowles, Holton, and Swanson (1998) in the form of statements or declarations that we typically hear from adult learners:

- I Need to Know What, Why, and How
- Involve Me in the Process of Decision Making
- Value My Experience
- Connect My Learning and My Life
- I Have My Own Reasons for Learning

In this book, we'll explore each of these areas and provide a variety of strategies for consideration by adult educators. One of the major goals that we set for ourselves as we put this book together was to provide an accessible, easy-to-implement guide for teaching adults—a book that you could easily take into the classroom with the idea of implementing one or more new teaching strategies. Readers of this text are encouraged to think of these strategies as a starting point for their own exploration, growth, and experimentation in meeting the needs of adult learners. Your students will appreciate the efforts that you are making to meet their needs as learners.

—CHERYL TOROK FLEMING
Assistant Dean for Teaching and Learning
College of Adult and Professional Studies
Indiana Wesleyan University

—J. BRADLEY GARNER
Assistant Dean for Teaching and Learning
College of Arts and Sciences
Indiana Wesleyan University

1

WHAT WOULD
THE EXPERTS SAY?

Most educators embrace their own preferred models and theories of classroom organization and instructional practice. These means and methods are generally based on a combination of concepts and ideas of the educator's own choosing, but are generally attributable to theories that have been developed by researchers and theorists over a number of years. Although specific theories and models come in and out of vogue over time, most possess some common kernels of thought and are founded on research-based perspectives on learner characteristics and preferences (Beaman 1998; Bedi 2004).

In this chapter, we will address some of the key theories and current models of adult learning using a case study approach. The reader is encouraged to read and reflect upon the case studies. They serve as a springboard for, and introduction to, the specific theories discussed in this section. Let's get started by reading case study 1.

CASE STUDY 1: THE TALKING HEAD

Dr. Miller walked quickly toward his classroom. In preparation for his 6:00 p.m. American history class, he mentally reviewed his lesson plan for the evening. However, the thought of the steadily decreasing number of students attending his class continued to nag at the corners of his mind. Despite the hours spent preparing his PowerPoint slides and lectures, Dr. Miller found his students less and less engaged in the class. Posting the slides and lecture notes on his website did not seem to help either. In fact, after he provided this help to his students, attendance in his class seemed to drop yet again. To make matters worse, those students who did come to class didn't seem interested in answering any of the questions posed by Dr. Miller. They preferred to look down at their notebooks until he answered the questions himself and moved on to the next point. Some students sat in the very back of the large lecture hall with their notebook computers open. Although they claimed to be taking notes, Dr. Miller was never sure exactly what those students were doing. "Students today seem to be so unmotivated," Dr. Miller sighed as he thought to himself. "Even the use of the PowerPoint technology does not seem to engage them."

Dr. Miller, a good friend of yours, has asked you for some advice. How would you respond?

ONLY TWENTY MORE SLIDES TO GO

The use of PowerPoint slides as the primary means of instruction with the students in Dr. Miller's class did not connect with their needs as adult learners. He probably created an environment where the students perceived that he cared more about getting through all his slides than he did assuring they gained an understanding of the instructional content. We may want to encourage Dr. Miller to reduce the use of PowerPoint slides and include more discussion, active learning, and problem solving in his classroom.

THE THEORY:
Knowles' Concepts and Characteristics of Adult Learners

Malcolm Knowles (1913–1997) is considered one of the great theorists and researchers in adult learning. He literally "wrote the book" on adult education. Knowles, long known as a key innovator for adult learning, distinguished between the learning needs of children (i.e., pedagogy) and adults (i.e., andragogy). In his classic work entitled, *The Adult Learner—A Neglected Species* (1984), Knowles described six key characteristics of adult learners:

1. Adults have a deep need to know "why they need to know."
2. Adults are task-oriented in their learning.
3. Adults bring to the learning situation a wide range of experiences.
4. Adults have a deep psychological need to be self-directed learners.
5. Adults learn best when the learning directly applies to their life situation.
6. Adults are motivated by internal pressures, such as self-esteem or quality of life.

These initial concepts set forth by Knowles have, in recent years, come under scrutiny and criticism from some quarters. For most practitioners, however, these key principles are a fundamental template for understanding adult learners. Merriam and Caffarella consider andragogy to be an enduring model for understanding the key concepts of adult learning theory and practice. They observe that "it does not give us the total picture, nor is it a panacea for fixing adult learning practices. Rather, it constitutes one piece of the rich mosaic of adult learning" (1999, 278).

As you read and examine each of the case studies, consider the degree to which the learning principles can be connected to the original work on andragogy done by Malcolm Knowles and his colleagues. Let's try another case study. Read case study 2.

CASE STUDY 2: STUDENT SEMINAR BLUES

Peter and Miguel walked slowly toward their Seminar for Elementary Teachers class at Northern Lights College. The sound of conversation and laughter emanated from the classroom as they approached.

Miguel: Peter, I've been trying for three weeks now to get enthused about this course, but I just can't seem to do it.

Peter: I know what you mean. Sitting through another one of those boring sessions led by some educational expert is almost more than I can take.

M: Don't get me wrong: I enjoy the opportunities to talk with other future teachers. But . . . well, we never seem to do much of that. Usually we just sit and listen, or have some goofy, childish games.

P: I agree, Miguel. The tables and chairs are so close together too. I feel uncomfortable. Just once, I wish someone would ask us what we would find valuable in these seminars.

M: Yes, I know. Who better than the students in this class would know what topics would be most interesting and helpful?

P: Well, I'm not wasting my time during this session. I have so much work to do . . . I brought along my laptop because I have a paper to write for another class. Let's just sit in the back by the door.

M: Sounds like they're getting started. I guess we better go in and get this over with.

What do the seminar planners need to know about self-directed learning?

SOMETHING NEEDS TO CHANGE

Self-directed learning may be just what the doctor ordered for this classroom. Peter and Miguel are probably expressing an opinion voiced by a majority of the students in the class. In fact, the teacher may be noticing the telltale signs of "lecture-induced mind paralysis" creeping into the class (see Garner 2007). This phenomenon is characterized by blank stares, drooping eyes, heads that appear too heavy to support their own weight, uncontrollable doodling, window/door gazing, compulsive clock watching, and occasional drooling.

The teacher would be well served by finding ways to more actively engage the students in their own learning by encouraging class discussion, dialogue, and problem-solving experiences that center around the real problems faced by educators in school settings. In any case, the students have expressed an important feeling held by many adult learners: the need to have more control and influence over their own learning.

THE THEORY:
Self–Directed Learning

Models of self-directed learning are largely based on the work of Tough (1991) and Brookfield (1985). Merriam and Caffarella (1999) indicate that many public schools, as well as colleges and universities, subscribe to the self-directed learning model in order to encourage students to become lifelong learners:

Although learning on one's own has been the primary mode of learning in adulthood through the ages, serious study of this phenomenon is relatively recent in comparison to other aspects of learning in adulthood, such as intelligence and participation. Why is there this apparent dichotomy between the prevalence of this learning mode and the lack of serious study for so long (Merriam and Caffarella 1999, 288)?

Cranton, in *Working with Adult Learners*, describes the process of self-directed learning as "the process of voluntarily engaging in a learning experience, being free to think or act as an individual during that experience, being free to reflect on that experience, and being able to discern change or growth as a result of the experience, regardless of the setting in which it occurs" (1992, 56). Isn't that what every teacher wants for all her students?

Merriam and Caffarella (1999), based on the work of Brookfield (1985) and Mezirow (1985), suggest that the goals of self-directed learning can be grouped into three basic categories: (1) to support the learner in becoming self-directed; (2) to encourage and support personal and social action as a result of self-directed learning; and (3) to assist the learner in becoming transformed into an individual with knowledge of self and the ability to reflect on one's actions and perspectives.

Within the literature on self-directed learning, three prominent models appear: linear, interactive, and instructional. The linear model closely mirrors more traditional approaches to learning, where learners are provided with key concepts upon which additional learning is based, while also encouraging learners to move in a stepwise fashion through the curriculum as they acquire new knowledge, skills, and dispositions. Interactive models focus more closely on the learner's own motivation, experiences, and environment for learning, as well as personality characteristics and thought processes. Finally, instructional models address how instruction may be organized in both formal and informal settings (see Merriam and Caffarella 1999).

Self-directed learning occurs when an individual makes a conscious choice to engage in the acquisition or refinement of new or currently held knowledge, skills, or dispositions. These learning opportunities, both formal and informal, could include coursework or degree programs, extensive reading on a particular topic, participation in seminars, music or art lessons, lectures, or workshops. As a result of participation in the chosen learning activity, the learner consciously changes his or her thoughts, viewpoints, opinions, or actions. In a self-directed experience, the learner is also able to describe or explain the changes he or she has made, as well as the effect these changes have on his or her life.

Self-directed learning activities provide the opportunity for the learner to make choices and to have some level of control over what to read, observe, say, or do. Consequently, the learner feels free to provide input, speak freely, express an opinion, and engage in an energetic and free-flowing discussion with other learners in the group. The learner also feels free to engage with the group leader or presenter, challenging the information provided or proposing new and different directions of thought (Cranton 1992).

Cranton (1992) suggests that since the learners become their own educators, the teacher should remain closely in tune with the emotional, social, intellectual, and skill needs of participating learners. Prior to even beginning to teach the class, the teacher should routinely and informally assess the needs of the group. Cranton lists the following questions to consider when planning for, or initiating, an instructional session:

1. Are the learners likely to have previous experience in self-directed learning?
2. Which components of the experience should be self-directed, and which should be other-directed?
3. How will the learning objectives be determined, and by whom?
4. Who will exercise control over the sequence of topics and activities?
5. What restrictions, if any, will be placed on the learners, such as time and place for learning to occur, required attendance, and specific learning strategies?
6. What learning resources and materials will be available to the learners?
7. How will the progress of the learners be assessed, and who will do this?
8. How will overall effectiveness of the learning experience be determined (Cranton 1992, 125–26)?

Finally, in order for self-directed learning to occur, the teacher should be willing to relinquish some aspects of control to the learners as they travel together through the learning process. While maintaining a firm belief in the ability of the learners to take responsibility for their own learning, the teacher remains a key figure in the total learning experience.

Are you ready for another one? Here's case study 3.

CASE STUDY 3: THE CLINICAL EXPERIENCE

Dr. Elli Patel arrived early to the clinical learning lab for the Southern College of Nursing in order to prepare for her newest student cohort. Dr. Patel looked forward to instructing her students, using the lecture room equipped with state-of-the-art technology. But she was even more interested in using the new lab in order to provide her students with immediate, hands-on experiences in diagnosing medical conditions and caring for patients. She was pleased to find the lab equipped with the most up-to-date equipment available for instructing students in the nursing program.

The interactive setting looked just like a hospital room, right down to the patients themselves! Heart monitors, blood pressure cuffs, thermometers, and blood sugar monitors all awaited the arrival of the students. Laptop computers sat alongside these traditional pieces of diagnostic equipment. Most surprising perhaps were the "patients"—human dummies. These patients were programmed with a variety of symptoms that provided simulated scenarios in which students applied the knowledge gained in lecture halls to actual medical situations. Following these clinical lab experiences, nursing students would participate in debriefing sessions. These experiences with the patients would be deconstructed and analyzed. Dr. Patel heard her new group of students approaching the classroom and eagerly anticipated the upcoming experiential teaching and learning that would soon take place in the "clinic."

What aspects of experiential learning are exemplified in Dr. Patel's classroom?

THIS LOOKS LIKE FUN

As a nursing student, wouldn't it be exciting to walk into this learning laboratory to begin practicing some of the skills you've been reading about in other introductory classes? Adult learners in Dr. Patel's class will be gaining experience that is directly related to their ultimate goal—to be nurses working with patients. We predict that the students in Dr. Patel's class are going to have a wonderful semester of learning experiences. The challenge for all teachers is to create learning environments that facilitate excitement on the part of their students: excitement about acquiring new skills and competencies that will pay long-term benefits.

THE THEORY:
Experiential Learning

Kolb's model of experiential learning finds its basis in the work of well-known theorists in the field of education, including Piaget, Dewey, and Lewin. The elements of Kolb's model include: (1) participation in concrete experiences; (2) observation and reflection about the experiences; (3) forming abstract concepts; and (4) testing those concepts in new situations. Kolb identified four specific types of skills or abilities required of a learner for maximum achievement utilizing experiential learning. These include: openness and willingness to involve oneself in new experiences, observational and reflective skills, analytical abilities, decision-making and problem-solving skills (see Kolb and Fry 1975; Merriam and Caffarella 1999).

Kolb's cyclical model allows learners to experience a constant building of reflective thought and action. Active experimentation in new situations encourages students to apply previously learned concepts, thus leading to reflective observation, changes and additions to previous knowledge, and plans for application of this new knowledge (Merriam and Caffarella 1999, 224). As we observed, the students in the nursing lab were given classroom experiences that were remarkably similar to those they would experience as nurses in a hospital. These experiences were both motivating and engaging. Consider how you might provide more realistic experiential learning experiences for your own students.

And now, case study 4.

CASE STUDY 4: HURRY TO CLASS!

Marie hurried across campus to her class on personal finance. She dared not arrive late as she was certain to miss something important. Professor Christman always began the class by asking students to share a newspaper or journal article pertinent to the topic of the day, and Marie had carefully prepared for her turn to share her article today. Marie had already used what she had learned in the personal finance course to create a new spreadsheet program to track expenditures. She shared it with her supervisor at Campus Corner Coffee and they chose to use the spreadsheet in the business!

How has Professor Christman used learner-centered psychological principles of education in planning for the personal finance course?

THIS IS USEFUL INFORMATION!

Marie is gaining some powerful information in her classes that directly impacts other parts of her life. She is seeking out ways to connect classroom teaching and assigned readings with her roles and responsibilities at Campus Corner Coffee. As a learner, Marie is the focus of what goes on in the classroom. There is a sense that she is more than a person who happens to fill a seat in the classroom on Tuesday and Thursday evenings. She is a real person with a real life and a real connection to the time and energy she is giving as an adult learner.

THE THEORY:
Learner-Centered Instructional Practices

The American Psychological Association identified fourteen learner-centered psychological principles pertaining to participants in the instructional process. These principles addressed not only internal characteristics of learners, but also external environmental factors or the context of learning. These factors, divided into four categories, were described as follows:

1. The Context of Learning
   a. Nature of the learning process: successful learners construct meaning from information and experience. They assume responsibility for their own learning and actively participate in the learning process.
   b. Goals of the learning process: setting and pursuing goals that are personally meaningful provides an important foundation for learning. These goals represent both personal and educational aspirations, as well as interests of the learner.
   c. Construction of knowledge: the ability to relate new information to existing knowledge promotes interest in continuing the learning process. By integrating this information with prior knowledge and understanding, learners connect and transfer new knowledge to new situations in a meaningful way.
   d. Strategic thinking: successful learners create and use a variety of thinking and reasoning strategies. These strategies assist learners in problem-solving and decision-making situations.
   e. Thinking about thinking: both critical and creative thinking skills play a role in the learning process. Using higher order thinking skills helps learners to reassess their personal goals, monitor their progress, and engage in reflective thinking processes.
   f. Context of learning: the setting or context in which learning occurs can enhance or detract from learning. These environmental factors include technology, culture, group influences, and instructional practices used by the teacher.

2. Motivational and Affective Factors

   a. Motivational and emotional influences on learning: learners' beliefs about themselves, as well as their internal motivation, play a significant role in learner success. Curiosity and mild anxiety can enhance learning, while self-doubt and worry interfere with learning and student performance.

   b. Intrinsic motivation to learn: creativity and curiosity of the learner contribute to the learner's continuing interest in the pursuit of knowledge and skills. Intrinsic motivation to learn is enhanced by connecting learning to real-world situations and personal interests, and allowing personal choice and control.

   c. Effects of motivation on effort: the willingness to put forth effort in order to master a subject indicates motivation to learn. Extended learner effort and guided practice reinforce the learner's commitment to work toward achievement of personal and educational goals.

3. Developmental and Social Factors

   a. Developmental influences on learning: individuals learn best when educators or trainers take into account the intellectual, emotional, and social characteristics of the learner. Presenting developmentally appropriate material in an interesting and enjoyable way supports the efforts of the learner and encourages active participation in the learning process.

b. Social influences on learning: interpersonal interactions also influence learning success. Opportunities to collaborate with other learners encourage the development of trusting and caring relationships within the group, and allow the student to experience enhanced personal well-being and a sense of belonging to the group.

4. Individual Differences

a. Individual differences in learning: attention to individual learning styles promotes a continuing desire to learn and an interest in the learning activities. Educators can help students improve upon and utilize their own learning modalities, and tap into new learning activities.

b. Learning and diversity: any group of individuals includes diversity in the form of ethnic, racial, linguistic, and social backgrounds. Careful attention to these differences promotes optimal opportunities for learning to occur, allowing individuals to feel respected and valued.

c. Standards and assessment: ongoing assessment of individual achievement and progress provides important feedback to learners. Educators can then utilize the information gained from assessments to adjust teaching techniques as needed, in order to appropriately challenge students and facilitate continued leaning.

Attention to these principles when planning instructional activities will support and encourage adult learners as they acquire new knowledge, skills, and dispositions. Specific learner-centered strategies include peer tutoring and coaching, cooperative learning activities, technology-based strategies, interdisciplinary projects, performance-based assessment, and opportunities for choice and self-monitoring (see Bonk 2004).

Now try your hand at another case study. Consider the situation created by Dr. Knolli.

> **Maslow's Hierarchy of Needs**
>
> Maslow's hierarchy of needs (as described in Slavin 2006) can be found in most introductory psychology textbooks, which were designed for students intending to pursue careers in the worlds of business, education, nursing, or ministry. The hierarchy includes basic human physiological needs such as freedom from hunger, absence of fear or threat, and the need to belong. As these needs are met, an individual begins to focus on higher level needs, such as the knowledge and understanding of situations and concepts, the appreciation of beauty, and the desire to realize one's own capabilities and strengths.

CASE STUDY 5: FEAR FACTOR

Dr. Knolli has presided over accounting classrooms at a local community college for five years. His name strikes fear into the hearts of his students. Nearly every student has a "Knolli story" to relate, and students new to the college are always warned about Dr. Knolli because he teaches a required course for accounting students. During one of his class sessions, a student asks a challenging question. Dr. Knolli turns angrily from the whiteboard, and proceeds to not only belittle the student, but then reminds her of his extensive history of credentials and publications. The other twenty students sit in stunned silence, looking down at their texts. By the end of the term, the students have learned to sit quietly, nodding their heads, asking few questions, and regurgitating back to Dr. Knolli what he wants to hear.

What changes to this classroom culture could you offer based upon Maslow's hierarchy of needs? (See sidebar.)

DO YOU HAVE ANY QUESTIONS?

Dr. Knolli has created a difficult classroom situation. The student's question was well intentioned and could have served as a great way to begin a classroom discussion. But Dr. Knolli allowed this interruption to serve as a way of devaluing a student's concerns and questions. The learner's needs were minimized in favor of Dr. Knolli's need to cover the material and stay on schedule.

One way to eliminate this occurrence from future classroom sessions would be to arrange the classroom schedule to include opportunities for dialogue and discussion. These are integral parts of the instructional process and can serve as diagnostic indicators of student understanding. (Readers are also encouraged to consider the "Exit Card" strategy found in chapter 2.)

THE THEORY:
Motivational and Affective Factors

The application of Maslow's hierarchy of needs to adult learning theory revolves around the importance of providing an atmosphere that is free from threat; where adult learners feel confident in expressing their own thoughts and ideas. In addition, adult learners should be encouraged to engage with the teacher in discussion, and to question and challenge information without fear of reprisal. Students who are unsure of their social or emotional safety in the classroom will tend to err on the side of safety, resulting in writing dull and uncreative papers and essays, learning material only to pass a test, and remaining silent during class discussions. In *Educational Psychology: Theory and Practice*, Slavin (2006) states,

A teacher who can put students at ease and make them feel accepted and respected as individuals is more likely (in Maslow's view) to help them become eager to learn for the sake of learning and willing to risk being creative and open to new ideas. If students are to become self-directed learners, they must believe that the teacher will respond fairly and consistently to them and that they will not be ridiculed or punished for honest errors (Slavin 2006, 320–21).

It would be a mistake to talk about safe spaces to learn without invoking the wisdom of Parker Palmer, the prototype of an educator who not only speaks the words but lives the life. Consider for a moment the picture of a typical adult learner in a college class—and the learning relationships that begin to grow and emerge during that class—as a journey of both heart and of mind. Palmer (1999), in his book *Let Your Life Speak: Listening for the Voice of Vocation*, offers the following advice on what can emerge as teachers and students collaborate and learn from one another:

The gift we receive on the inner journey is the knowledge that ours is not the only act in town. Not only are there other acts out there, but some of them are even better than ours, at least occasionally! We learn that we need not carry the whole load but that we can share it with others, liberating us and empowering them. We learn that sometimes we are free to lay the load down altogether. The great community asks us to do only what we are able and trust the rest to other hands (Palmer 1999, 89).

This picture requires that we rethink the dynamics of the classroom. Certainly, the professor carries a major responsibility for creating the space for learning and sharing knowledge. At the same time, however, the master teacher will create places and opportunities for students to step into a role of leadership, facilitation, and shared responsibility for what happens in the classroom. How might you share varied aspects of the learning that occurs in your classroom?

In addition to the factors already discussed, we know that adult learners bring to the mix a host of other concerns and life situations that can interfere with learning. These include family or social situations, job responsibilities, health or financial worries, and issues related to other coursework. Instructors would do well to remain mindful of these other concerns and life situations when assigning coursework, crafting late-work policies, or addressing lack of student preparation for class.

To begin this process, consider the following questions about the atmosphere, culture, and expectations for your own classroom:

1. What would my students say about my willingness to engage in dialogue about issues that I feel strongly about, but that also invite a variety of opposing opinions and perspectives?
2. Are there times that I have responded to a student's question or comment in a way that was unintentionally hurtful or

minimizing? Did I make an effort to reconcile that relationship with a follow-up conversation?

3. Is my classroom a place where I take risks in learning and encourage my students to do the same? What are some ways that this approach to learning could be evidenced?

4. When the time comes to talk with a student about a classroom issue (e.g., excessive absences, plagiarism, poor overall performance), do I engage in that conversation in a manner that sends the message of concern while also respecting the student's personal dignity?

5. What are some of the other possible indicators and criteria for a safe learning space?

And now, here's another scenario to consider.

CASE STUDY 6: PART OF THE TEAM

This was the last evening of class, but Michael's hands were clammy as he and his three presentation partners waited their turn in the corridor outside the classroom. This final evening revolved around the presentation of team projects, and Michael and his partners would soon engage in a debate scenario on global warming, thus completing their final project for the course. All his team members had worked diligently on the project, prepared extensive notes and a final written paper, and endlessly rehearsed their roles in preparation for the evening. Michael could most certainly say that he had learned quite a lot about global warming; in fact, some of his opinions of the subject had undergone radical shifts. Michael even decided to make some changes in his own life based on what he had learned. Now it was time for Michael and his team to present the debate scenario to the class, for which they would receive both instructor and peer feedback, and their final project grade. The door opened, and Michael and his team entered the classroom to begin their presentation . . .

What aspects of transformative learning would be at play in the team presentation?

THIS WAS MORE THAN AN ASSIGNMENT!

Sometimes there's a tendency, even in jest, to contrast the world of the classroom with the real world. The goal of classroom learning should be to transform students to the extent that they are more willing and able to engage the "real world" in new and different ways. This can be accomplished by making a conscious effort to create intersections between the learners (and their unique collection of needs, strengths, gifts, and talents), the instructional content (with intentional efforts to provide handles and touch points that underscore relevance and usefulness), and the needs of the world (and there are many). As theologian Frederick Buechner observed in *Wishful Thinking: A Seeker's ABC*, "True vocation is the place where your deep gladness meets the world's deep need" (1993, 119). An integral part of the instructional process is to help students find their deep gladness and explore the world's deep need. That exploration can transform the student and change the world. Be that teacher!

THE THEORY:
Transformative Learning

According to Merriam and Caffarella (1999), the transformative learning model, first devised by Freire (1993) and Mezirow (1991) involves three key concepts: (1) the nature of life experience that is central to adult learning; (2) critical reflection processes; and (3) the connection between adult development and the transformative process. This model begins with a learner who possesses an established set of values and assumptions based on his or her experiences, set within a social context, and involving a learning situation that may be either formal or informal.

The transformative process begins as a result of a situation experienced by the learner, in which he or she confronts a dilemma that is incongruent with his or her previous life experiences. The learner may feel challenged to engage in critical thinking in order to reexamine his or her values through a reflective process. This, according to Cranton, "results in the reformulation of a meaning perspective to allow a more inclusive, discriminating, and integrative understanding of one's experience" (1992, 151).

For the educator, it is critically important not to rigidly impose his or her ideas and perspectives on the learner. The teacher, in the role of a learning coach or facilitator, simply provides the venue and the conditions for learners to engage in their own introspective processes, examine their own assumptions, and arrive at new implications for thought or action. Other possible steps to consider include: (1) providing activities or guidance to learners to assist in this introspective process; (2) supporting learners in this analysis; (3) encouraging learners to engage in an examination of their previous assumptions; (4) providing a safe environment for challenging and questioning to occur; (5) assisting learners to integrate new ideas into their set of values and perspectives; and (6) facilitating the transfer of these new ideas to other environments (Cranton 1992; Merriam 2001; Merriam and Caffarella 1999). Educators should keep in mind that transformative learning takes time, and must include praxis, or putting into practical action what one has learned. Transformative learning can be an important vehicle for personal or social change. With these concepts in mind, educators are cautioned to consider the social-emotional and ethical aspects of transformative learning prior to engaging in activities which support this type of learning.

Specific classroom activities which could be used to facilitate the transformative process include journal writing, simulations and case studies, critical incidents, role-playing, metaphors, personal biographical sketches, life histories, narratives, visioning, and both small and large group discussions (Cranton 1999; Merriam 2001; Merriam and Caffarella 1999).

And now consider the final scenario.

CASE STUDY 7: CONSTRUCTING KNOWLEDGE

The animated conversation among the members of the Department of Business and Management quieted as Dr. Anna Zimmermann called the department meeting to order. After quickly working through the agenda of "Old Business" items, Dr. Zimmermann introduced Dr. James Cho, a colleague from Undergraduate Studies in Education. Dr. Cho would share some of the most effective instructional techniques in his repertoire, which he described as "constructivist methods." As the discussion progressed, Dr. Cho involved the Business and Management faculty as he demonstrated the techniques for the group. Although some members of the department seemed interested, even enthusiastic, others demonstrated skepticism and even hostility! Let us listen to some comments from three colleagues who were part of this group:

John Reese: "I think this interactive stuff is a bunch of garbage! How can I use these techniques in teaching accounting? I lecture and demonstrate the problems, then have the students work similar problems at their seats."

Ami Srinivasan: "It all sounds interesting—the methods Dr. Cho discussed about involving the students in small groups, and trying to find out what they already know about the subject. But how might that work in a finance class? I'm not sure."

Alan Trist: "I stopped by Dr. Cho's class one day. The students were working with partners and discussed their past experiences in education. When Dr. Cho gave a signal, they all switched partners. There was a lot of noise and laughter. It looked like a lot of fun . . . but I wonder how much learning was really going on in there?"

What would Dr. Cho tell these faculty members about constructivist theory and methods?

BUILDING A LEARNING EXPERIENCE

Have you ever sat up in bed in the middle of the night startled by an insight or the answer to a pressing dilemma or life-question?

Learning often occurs in that fashion. Pieces of information, isolated concepts, or disparate situations come together to form a whole that is greater than the sum of the parts. This process of constructing knowledge is an approach to teaching and learning that is becoming increasingly popular and effective with adult learners. As you will undoubtedly notice, in this text we will consistently argue for a classroom that is active and alive with dialogue, disagreement, and discovery as faculty and students search for understanding together.

THE THEORY:
Constructivism

Constructivism refers to not just one, but a combination of similar concepts about the ways in which humans gain knowledge and develop new ideas. Constructivist theory emphasizes the relationship between human knowledge and social experience, with shared inquiry as an essential component of learning. A constructivist approach to planning for classroom instruction will provide ways for students to tie new ideas to previous life experiences, constructing and reorganizing current knowledge to add meaning to subsequently acquired ideas and new experiences (Apple and Teitelbaum 2001). According to Slavin, teachers can facilitate the construction of learning by "teaching in ways that make information meaningful and relevant, by giving students opportunities to discover or apply ideas themselves, and by teaching students to be aware of and consciously use their own strategies for learning" (2006, 243).

The work of Dewey, Bruner, Piaget, Vygotsky, and Gardner represents the theorists most commonly associated with concepts of constructivist learning. Constructivism, however, also contains component concepts from fields such as philosophy, psychology, and science. In a constructivist framework, individuals continually reformulate their schemas, or bodies of personal knowledge, based on newly acquired information and experienced events. This process of developing knowledge by making meaning from new experiences is influenced and driven by personal introspection and reflection, as well as by social interactions (see Slavin 2006; Walker and Lambert 1995).

Walker and Lambert (1995, 17–19) elucidate the following principles and key descriptors of constructivism:

1. Knowledge and beliefs are formed within the learner.
2. Learners personally imbue experiences with meaning.
3. Learning activities should cause learners to gain access to their experiences, knowledge, and beliefs.
4. Learning is a social activity that is enhanced by shared inquiry.
5. Reflection and metacognition are essential aspects of constructing knowledge and meaning.
6. Learners play a critical role in assessing their own learning.
7. The outcomes of the learning process are varied and often unpredictable.

With this information in mind, what does a constructivist classroom look like? What means of instruction would a constructivist teacher employ? There are several key processes and approaches that will guide the instructional process. First, learning in a constructivist classroom often takes the form of interaction and collaboration among participants. For this reason, there will be a strong emphasis on active learning techniques (e.g., dyad/triad/small group discussions, group projects, experiential field work).

Second, since a constructivist approach to learning is based upon accessing previous knowledge, the teacher should provide opportunities for students to reflect upon prior knowledge and experiences, and to engage in both personal reflection and group discussion. This provides a foundation upon which new knowledge can be built.

Third, acquisition of knowledge should be student-centered, with the teacher serving in the role of providing basic content knowledge to ground the subject under discussion. In addition, the teacher should offer guidance and assistance in the acquisition of knowledge in the form of prompts, questions, suggested tasks and resources, and challenges. Vygotsky used the term *scaffolding*, or mediated learning, to refer to the role of the teacher as a support available to students as they engage in complex, realistic, or challenging tasks (as cited in Slavin 2006).

Fourth, learning in a constructivist classroom is not based on cramming for a test, or memorization of long lists of dates, vocabulary terms, or historical events. Rather, students need to engage deeply with the subject matter in order to develop a thorough understanding of the concepts. The teacher should make opportunities available for students to dig into the course concepts rather than focusing on covering the topics. Learning occurs as students find ways to apply bodies of knowledge and determine their interrelationships through the demands and expectations of assigned tasks.

Fifth, rather than basing student achievement and assessment on just a few tests, constructivist educators embrace the idea of multiple and varied means of assessing student learning. In a constructivist classroom, students are offered many ways to demonstrate their understanding of and engagement with the course material.

Finally, constructivist learning environments present students with opportunities to apply new knowledge to their own life experiences. Student motivation is augmented when students view learning tasks as relevant, important, useful, and applicable to their own life situations and circumstances (Vermette et al. 2001).

SOME CLOSING THOUGHTS

Most educators would do well to gain an understanding of some of the underlying theories and models of adult learning. While many such models exist in the literature, each individual forms his or her own educational philosophy, which molds actual practice. This chapter used case studies as a means to introduce and illustrate seven different models and theorists of adult learning:

1. Knowles' Concepts and Characteristics of Adult Learners
2. Mezirow and Brookfield's Self-Directed Learning Model
3. Kolb's Experiential Learning Theory
4. American Psychological Association's Learner-Centered Principles of Education
5. Maslow's Hierarchy of Motivational and Affective Needs
6. Mezirow and Freire's Transformative Learning
7. Constructivist Learning Theory

Knowledge and understanding of adult learners forms a strong foundation for planning effective educational programs aimed at adults. Active adult learners seek out learning experiences in order to cope with life-changing events. Additionally, adult learners need to be able to tie new learning to past experiences, and to see the practical value and use of this learning.

Optimal learning experiences seem to be those that are set in socially and emotionally safe environments, valuing the learners' previous experiences and involving participants in dialogue with others. Finally, allowing self-direction to occur while providing some form of challenge to existing thoughts and ideas can further strengthen the link between new learning and previous life experiences.

2
I NEED TO KNOW WHAT, WHY, AND HOW

The only kind of learning which significantly influences behavior is self-discovered or self-appropriated learning—truth that has been assimilated in experience.

—Carl Rogers

Look into the faces of the students sitting before you. They have come to your classroom from many directions for a wide variety of reasons. Consider, for example, the criteria used by the National Center for Educational Statistics (NCES) to define an "adult learner." According to NCES, adult learners (who fall into the category of nontraditional students) meet one or more of the following criteria:

- Delay enrollment (do not enter postsecondary education in the same calendar year that he or she finished high school).
- Attend part-time for at least part of the academic year.
- Work full-time (35 hours or more per week) while enrolled.
- Are considered financially independent for purposes of determining eligibility for financial aid.
- Have dependents other than a spouse (usually children, but sometimes others).

- Are single parents (either not married or married but separated and have dependents).
- Do not have a high school diploma (completed high school with a GED or other high school completion certificate or did not finish high school).

By definition, this group of students is a picture of diversity. Within this heterogeneous group of learners, we find a variety of reasons for student willingness to extend themselves beyond the basics of timing, family responsibilities, financial considerations, and previous educational experiences. From these varied vantage points they are drawn together to engage in learning. And they bring with them the questions *what*, *why*, and *how*?

THE "WHAT" QUESTIONS: LEARNING OUTCOMES

Good teaching starts with the destination in mind. Before beginning the journey, both teacher and learner must have a clear idea about where they are headed. This maxim is particularly relevant to the adult learner. There is an old, and overly used, rhetorical adage that asks the question, "How do you eat an elephant?" The answer, of course, is "One bite at a time." This example begs the question that is an eternal challenge to teachers in all education and training environments: how much is enough (or too much, or not enough) content to cover over the course of a semester? Consider these facts:

- You can't teach your students all there is to know about your discipline;

- You can't teach your students everything that you know about your discipline;
- You are the person in the best position to systematically identify the direction, focus, and quantity of content that will be covered.

Take seriously your power and ability to determine the most cogent and significant knowledge, skills, and dispositions that you will emphasize over the course of the semester. Take the time to communicate these outcomes to your students.

The National Council on Accreditation in Teacher Education (NCATE) is the organization that is primarily responsible for assessing and accrediting teacher education programs in the United States. As part of their framework, prospective teachers are expected to demonstrate competencies in the areas of knowledge, skills, and dispositions. These three categories of performance can also provide a relevant and meaningful way of thinking about the kinds of learning outcomes that can be articulated for the college classroom. Consider these dimensions when thinking about the competencies that you wish your students to acquire in the courses you teach:

Knowledge

It's an awareness of empirical research and information in the field of study, the ability to engage in critical inquiry, and an awareness of key discipline-specific facts, truths, and principles.

Skills

Skills are application of knowledge in a variety of contexts, including prescribed proficiencies and techniques that can be selected and applied appropriately in varied settings, and under varied circumstances.

Dispositions

These are habitual inclinations, tendencies, values, commitments, and professional ethics that influence behaviors, choices, and courses of action.

Examine the outcomes that are identified for student learning in your courses. Do these outcomes consider the varied aspects of knowledge, skills, and dispositions? In what ways could you modify these course objectives to mirror these competencies?

THE "WHY" QUESTIONS: RELEVANCE

Adult learners are anxious to know *why* they are being asked to master course-prescribed content. In the book *Schools That Learn*, Kallick (2000) provides the following illustrative framework that helps teachers analyze what they expect of their students, and helps students understand the three different types of knowledge that learners must acquire.

Imagine that you have a teenage son who is old enough to get a driver's license—and you are a little nervous about it. You drive him to the licensing agency to take the multiple-choice written test on state driving laws. When he returns with a big grin to tell you that he scored well, you are pleased and relieved. At least he knows the shape of a stop sign, the speed limit in a school zone, and the need to yield to pedestrians. He has proven his mastery of *formal knowledge*: he knows (or knows where to find) the academic, explicit, codified facts that any expert would need at his or her fingertips.

But are you ready to turn him loose with an automobile? Probably not. Eventually, after further hours of instruction behind the wheel, he passes the full-performance driving test. He proudly brings home his provisional driver's license. Now he's demonstrated *applicable knowledge*: the ability to transfer information into action, even in situations that are less than routine. Under a variety of conditions, he has the proficiency he needs to produce results.

You congratulate him, and he immediately asks for the keys to the car. What do you do now? The tests—both the written and the performance test—are inadequate in themselves. All they show is that he knows how to pass the tests.

Formal tests, even good ones, are not enough to assess learning authentically. Before your son can drive the car (or at least mine) alone, he must also show signs of *longitudinal knowledge*: the basic capability for acting effectively over time in a way that leads to ongoing improvement, effectiveness, and innovation (Kallick 2000, 186–87).

Quite often, learners want to make the leap over formal knowledge and head straight to applicable knowledge. Formal knowledge (e.g. information, factual content) is almost always a perquisite to other higher forms of learning. Consider talking with your students about the design of the course and the ways in which formal knowledge, applicable knowledge, and longitudinal knowledge are integrated within your course planning. Taking the time to provide these linkages will assist your students in understanding the flow and sequence of the learning that lies ahead.

THE "HOW" QUESTIONS: PEDAGOGY

Orienteering can be defined as "a running sport involving navigation with a map and compass . . . The competition is a timed race in which individual participants use a special purpose map and a magnetic compass to navigate through diverse terrain (often wooded) and visit, in sequence, control points that are indicated on the map" (Wikpedia, n.d.). Doesn't that sound like what faculty members and students do every semester (e.g., run a timed race, use a special purpose map, navigate through difficult terrain, and [hopefully] reach a prescribed destination)? In *Greater Expectations: A New Vision for Learning as a Nation Goes to College* (AACU 2002, 78), this connection between orienteering and learning outcomes was expanded in the following ways:

Orienteering Principles	Orienteering & Teaching
Orienteers use an accurate, detailed map and a compass	Accurate, detailed "maps" and curricula identify student outcomes
Novices go through a simple course and proceed to a more difficult challenge	Students progress through developmental learning stages as they acquire new knowledge, skills, and dispositions
A standard orienteering course includes a starting point, a series of control points, and a finish	Coursework includes a variety of stages and formats for assessing the quality of student performance and their ultimate mastery of course content

Imagine that your time with the students sitting in your classroom is a wonderful journey into a land of understanding, learning, and growth. The final destination is important—but so is the journey. Savor the content and the process.

Tools of the Trade

A primary consideration in working with adult learners is the organization and delivery of instruction. The following are some organizational structures that will help you think through the process for the design of engaging learning experiences that help your students answer the questions *what*, *why*, and *how*.

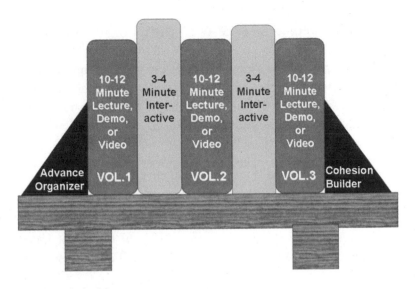

The Bookshelf Strategy

The Bookshelf model provides students with an immediate opportunity "to practice what you are preaching" (Smith et al. 2005). This approach assures that class presentations give students an opportunity to process their new learning and engage in critical thinking.

As depicted in the graphic above, each class begins with an advance organizer. Advance organizers are a collection of strategies that set the stage for instruction by advising learners of the topics, content, and focus of a class presentation. Based upon the early work of Ausabel, a body of research has revealed that learning increases dramatically when students are provided with a scaffold or framework that defines the nature of the learning experience. Advance organizers might include:

- A provocative question
- A famous quotation
- A story or news item

- A jointly developed "K-W-L" chart—i.e., what we know (K), what we want to learn (W), what we have learned (L); (See page 53 for a more detailed description of this strategy.)
- A video clip, news article, picture, song, or quotation
- Any thought-provoking introduction that hooks the learner and encourages students to want to know more about the topic of discussion
- An acrostic (An acrostic is a poem or series of lines in which certain letters, usually the first in each line, form a name, motto, or message when read in sequence.) Remember, for example, when you were in fourth grade and were asked to remember the names of the Great Lakes (HOMES) or the colors in a rainbow (ROY G. BIV). These acrostics helped you retain this information. Provide your students with the opportunity to create their own acrostics as organizational and learning aids.
- A graphic organizer—A graphic organizer is a visual strategy (e.g., flow chart, visual/topical outline) to help students remember important concepts and organize their thinking about varied interrelated concepts. To see the variety of graphic organizers that can be created, do a quick search on the Web for "graphic organizers."

The selected advance organizer is followed by a series of interspersed segments of lecture (i.e., 10–12 minutes in length) and discussions/video clips/demonstrations (i.e., 3–4 minutes in length). When thinking about the flow of instruction, consider strategies that will encourage students to interact, discuss the content, clarify their understandings, and generate questions or concerns that may arise.

As we proceed through this chapter, you will see several examples of interactive strategies that can be applied in this portion of the instructional process. For example, one very powerful strategy is "Paired Verbal Fluency" (Garmston and Wellman 2002). This strategy starts with putting each student with a dialogue teammate. When the clock starts, Team Member 1 starts talking about the topic at hand. He continues this monologue for 60 seconds. At the end of this minute, Team Member 2 begins to talk, not repeating any of the information shared by his partner. Team Member 2 continues for one minute. Then it's Team Member 1's turn again; this time for 30 seconds of uninterrupted talking. And finally, Team Member 2 gets a final chance to talk for his allocated 30 seconds. This activity is highly energizing and the students are usually amazed at how much they have learned and can remember. And as students articulate what they have learned, they are engaging in a powerful way of promoting the retention of new information and placing it into context.

THE RULE OF TEN AND TWO

Another consideration in the planning of a class lesson is the Rule of Ten and Two (Garmston and Wellman 1999). This approach balances the time allocated for teacher talk and student processing. The Rule of Ten and Two states that for every ten minutes the teacher talks, students should be allocated two minutes to process the presented information and concepts.

Application Techniques for the Rule of Ten and Two

Often, the challenge of teaching is not delivering the lecture, but finding ways of creating an engaged learning environment in which students have the opportunity to process new information and wrestle with the concepts and ideas that have been presented. The following are some ways of accomplishing this task.

Group Response Cards

This strategy combines small group consensus building and the opportunity to gain a sense of the total group's response to issues of discussion. Each group of 3–5 students is provided with a series of response cards (e.g., Agree, Disagree, Not Sure). The faculty member then presents a scenario or problem for the class to consider and discuss in small groups. At the signal, groups are asked to display their response cards. In this way, the faculty member can survey the responses and ask the groups to state their reasons for their chosen response.

This approach, of course, can be upgraded into a more technological framework by using one of the many personal response systems that are now on the market. This software provides students with the opportunity to respond to informational and opinion questions which are then tabulated and displayed for discussion and review. Or, at the other end of the continuum, you could choose to make homemade white boards and ask the groups to write their responses. In any case, the goal is involvement and engagement in the learning process.

Round the Clock Learning Partners

In larger classes, the faculty member may present students with a line drawing of a clock indicating times between 1:00 and 12:00. Each student must make appointments with twelve different classmates, corresponding with the hours on the clock. To introduce a time of interaction or discussion, the instructor simply tells the class to "Find your 2:00 partner and talk about . . . " (Garmston and Wellman 1999).

Seasonal Learning Partners

In smaller classes, the same strategy is used with one minor modification. The students are given a paper with the four seasons of the year and are asked to make appointments with four other people corresponding to the seasons of the year (Garmston and Wellman 1999).

Voting

In this strategy the instructor asks students to express their thoughts on topics that may involve controversy or differences of opinion by standing in response (i.e., if you agree with this position, please stand now) or by showing thumbs up/thumbs down (if you agree give a thumbs up; if you disagree, give a thumbs down; if you feel very strongly, wiggle your thumb as you vote or use both hands).

Exit Cards

Davis (2001) describes a procedure for encouraging students to engage in ongoing reflection about their learning. Exit cards provide a strategy for students to process what they are learning and apply that information to their chosen discipline of study. On a weekly basis, students are asked to complete a 5 x 8 card which contains three questions: *What?* (i.e., designed to elicit a summary of the main points that were discussed and reviewed during the week); *So what?* (i.e., the relevance of the topic); and, *Now what?* (i.e., relate that content to their lives, learning, and future roles and responsibilities).

Discussion Museum

This activity addresses learning styles, provides a structure for discussion, and keeps responses focused. Introverted students have time to prepare thoughts before writing or speaking. Students develop questioning skills and interact with peers. The steps in this process are as follows:

1. Write pithy quotes, interesting ideas, or questions on large pieces of paper. They are then displayed on the walls in the room.
2. Ask students to read each paper, then write their responses in silence. Use a timer or signal to move students to the next paper. Establish a few ground rules:
   a. Each person must respond to ___ number of items.
   b. Responses must be more than "I agree" or "Yes."
   c. The room must remain quiet during this activity.
3. Divide the class into groups and distribute the large papers among the groups. Ask each group to read and summarize the written reflections on the paper assigned to the group, and to prepare 3–4 questions regarding the responses on the paper.

4. Ask each group to verbally debrief. Allow time for a class discussion.

Speed Discussion

This activity provides students with an opportunity to interact and process course-related information. This activity is fast-paced and allows sharing of different viewpoints in a short time period. The process for implementation of the speed discussion is as follows:

1. Create a list of 2–4 questions for discussion that relate to course content.
2. Arrange the seats in the room so that the desks/chairs face each other in two long rows.
3. Allow two minutes of talk time for each student to discuss with the student that they are facing.
4. After two minutes, students on one side of the row shift to the seat to their right.
5. Allow two minutes of talk time with new partners.
6. Repeat as time permits.
7. When the large group re-convenes, discuss/summarize ideas that surfaced during this time.
8. Ask students to process the responses by considering several clarifying questions:
   a. What opinions surprised you?
   b. With whom do you agree?
   c. With whom do you disagree?

SOME CLOSING THOUGHTS

The process of instruction begins with your thoughts and planning about what you will do and say when you step into the learning environment. This begins with the realization that your students will often have some difficult questions and will indeed want to know what, why, and how. To review:

1. Begin with the end in mind: what will your students be able to do, understand, communicate, appreciate, demonstrate, etc., at the conclusion of the class session or learning experience?
2. Why should this knowledge, skill, or disposition be part of the curriculum?
3. How can you design a learning experience that promotes mastery and understanding?
4. After the teaching experience, process what occurred, the outcomes that were met (or not), and make necessary adjustments for the next steps of the journey.

3

INVOLVE ME IN
THE PROCESS OF
DECISION MAKING

Small groups of aspiring adults who desire to keep their minds fresh and vigorous; who begin to learn by confronting pertinent situations; who dig down into the reservoirs of their secondary facts; who are led in the discussion by teachers who are also seekers after wisdom and not oracles: this constitutes the setting for adult education, the modern quest for life's meaning.

— Eduard Lindeman

Think for a few moments about your classroom learning environment and the degree to which you involve the learners in making decisions about the instructional process. Consider the following guiding questions:

1. To what extent, and in what ways, do you communicate to participating learners that you value and respect their opinions and ideas?
2. What is the tone of your response to questions and challenges?
3. Do you offer learners opportunities to make choices about the ways in which they learn and are evaluated?
4. Are you asking questions that are designed to assist students in clarifying their own learning?
5. What kinds of alterations and adjustments have you made in the past in response to student concerns and ideas?

A growing body of research illustrates and clarifies the ways in which adult learners differ from their traditional counterparts. In *Researching Adult Learners' Lives*, Appleby (2004) suggests the importance of involvement in instructional decision making as a key component:

Negotiation and control were frequently cited by adult learners as important in providing a sense of self-respect, increasing confidence and allowing them to create a pace of learning where they felt they could succeed. Learners identified strongly with delivery (Appleby 2004, 22).

Despite the overriding principle of adult learning which indicates that learners need to be involved in making decisions about their own learning, a significant caveat must be addressed. Vella (1994) suggests that many adult learners may not be adequately prepared for that level of instructional autonomy. There may be several reasons for this self-imposed feeling of inadequacy, including a sense of awe and distance from the teacher, lack of previous experience in the design of their own learning, lack of awareness of the alternatives that may be considered, and a difficulty in effectively engaging in the process of developing and selecting alternative paths of action.

If adult learners are to be actively involved in decision making about their own learning, then faculty members must develop a process that will allow them to think through the alternatives in a systematic manner. Adult learners should also be encouraged to make adjustments and revisions to their initial plans, as they gain a better working knowledge of how the content area relates to their own needs and interests.

One of the authors of this text was recently teaching a summer graduate course to a group of practicing elementary and secondary school teachers. In preparation for the class, a series of assignments had been created and included in the course syllabus. These were assignments typically included in graduate level coursework: literature reviews, analysis of research studies from professional literature, and development of a research-based action plan for incorporating the course concepts into their classroom practice.

During one class period, a student rather sheepishly raised her hand and asked if she could gain further clarification about the course assignments, evoking a visible sense of interest on the part of the other students. As the discussion developed, it was apparent that the class had been discussing these assignments and the student who originally raised the question was their elected and willing representative. The conversation was highly constructive and informative; and as a result, a collaborative process led to the development of a new assignment . . . one that was more appropriate than the original assignment.

In retrospect, the original assignments, although reasonable and valuable, were more esoteric than practical. The instructor had failed to recognize that this group of adult learners came to class interested in acquiring new information, but with one important caveat: they, as teachers, wanted to acquire information that they could translate into practice within their own classrooms. This is not to suggest that assignments are always up for grabs! At the same time, neither are they sacred. The skillful teacher learns to strike a balance between the two extremes.

THE SYLLABUS AS A FOUNDATION FOR LEARNING AND DECISION MAKING

A staple of higher education is the creation of course syllabi. As routine as this process may sound, or even become, the development of a thorough, complete, and well-conceived course syllabus can provide the groundwork for a successful semester of learning. According to Littlefield (1999), a high-quality syllabus fulfills these functions:

- Sets the tone for the course—A well developed course syllabus sends the important message that the faculty member has given serious thought to course organization and delivery. A syllabus that is attractive, well organized, and that captures the interest of students from the first day of class will pay benefits throughout the semester.
- Motivates students to set high goals for themselves—If students sense your excitement, passion, and commitment to the content of the course, they are more likely to stretch themselves to achieve and produce. Consider your syllabus as an invitation to your students—an invitation to give their best efforts and to get your best efforts. Expect great things from your students and give them great teaching in exchange.
- Serves as a planning tool—A high quality syllabus sets forth the teacher's game plan for the semester. As you go through the process of developing your course syllabus, you are additionally afforded the opportunity to plan your instructional strategies for the semester.
- Offers a structure for student work—You are competing for the time, interest, and energies of your students. A well-conceived syllabus communicates your expectation that students will invest themselves in meeting the learning requirements of your course. This provision also encourages students to look ahead and plan effective ways to complete assigned tasks.
- Helps faculty plan and meet course requirements and expectations—Planning time spent in advance of the semester (e.g., order of approaching topics, timing of assignments, planning in regard to instructional activities)

will pay dividends in the quality of your teaching. You have a sense of where you're headed and can lead your students' learning in that direction.

- Provides a contractual arrangement between faculty and students—Any disagreements that may arise concerning grading practices, due dates, and attendance policies can be referred back to the stated course policies and procedures.
- Becomes a portfolio artifact for promotion—As time passes and you prepare for promotion and the preparation of a portfolio, course syllabi serve as a means for documenting the quality of your teaching and the ways in which you addressed the learning needs of your students.

As you plan for the semester ahead, consider using this Syllabus Preparation Checklist as a template for the types of information that you include. However, remember our earlier discussion of orienteering and the ways in which there may be multiple paths to reaching the final destination of the journey that you are taking with your students.

SYLLABUS PREPARATION CHECKLIST

General Information: This introductory section of the syllabus provides basic information such as the course title, section number(s), classroom location, dates and times of class meetings, faculty contact information (e.g., telephone numbers, email addresses), required texts and course materials, and your office hours.

Course Rationale: This is your opportunity to share the reasons why this course is critically important and how the content connects with the life and learning experiences of your students.

Your Passion and Purpose in Teaching This Course: In this section of the syllabus, share your personal and professional passion for this course and the things that will be taught and learned. Share your heart and your faith with your students.

Course Objectives: Articulate the knowledge, skills, and dispositions that you believe are important for your students to master over the course of this semester.

Topical Schedule: How do you plan to approach the breadth and depth of the topics that comprise this area of study? In this section of the syllabus, provide your students with a dated schedule of the topics that you will be sharing and learning about on this semester-long adventure.

Course Reading: Students are not genetically and naturally inclined to read required course materials. Through your prompting and systematic planning, however, they can be encouraged to see the value of reading along as they are learning.

Course Products: Students need to know in detail what assignments you expect them to produce this semester, the parameters of those assignments, and when they are due. Although some may choose to procrastinate, it's still important to provide specific dates for task completion.

Assessment Scheme: "Will this be on the test?" is a common refrain of the college classroom. Prepare in advance for the assessment strategies that you will use (e.g., quizzes and examinations, research papers, group projects, presentations, online activities). Provide your students with information on these tasks and their relative levels of importance (e.g., point values).

Course and University Policies: What are the policies and procedures that your students need to understand as they enter this course? Examples include attendance procedures, reasonable and acceptable absences, and consequences for cheating or academic dishonesty. Spell these out in your syllabus or give reference points so students remain well informed.

Motivational Thoughts: As an added touch, consider the use of graphics and text boxes with quotes that connect with your course and teaching.

Additional Resources and Assistance: Provide students with resources of how to get additional assistance they may need (appropriate internet links and campus resources) to assist in their learning.

TOOLS OF THE TRADE

The K-W-L Chart

The development of a K-W-L chart is a process that provides students with an opportunity to identify what they know (K), what they want to learn (W), and what they have learned (L) about a particular topic or content area (see Ogle 1986). In a teaching situation, students might be asked to create a number of post-it-note entries that correspond to the K, W, and L categories. This could be done individually or in a small group. Additionally, it may be helpful to keep the chart posted to provide an opportunity for students to add new entries to the K and W categories, or move post-it-notes to the L category as new pieces of skill, knowledge, or disposition are learned.

A Unique Approach: The A La Carte Syllabus

Imagine that you are extremely hungry and have just been given the opportunity to partake of a meal at one of your favorite restaurants. The food at this eatery is extraordinary! You've decided to throw caution to the wind and ignore the everyday concerns about calories, fat content, and carbohydrates. As the waiter approaches, you struggle with what to order because there are several items on the menu that you really enjoy. You hesitate, and then describe your dilemma to the waiter. Much to your surprise, he invites you to simply pick and choose from a variety of meal options based upon your own personal preferences. You choose a meal that meets your own needs and preferences. Let the meal begin (even though you may be sorry tomorrow)!

Consider this illustration in relation to course design and student learning. As teachers, we all strive to provide instructional opportunities that will maximize the degree to which our students gain new information, understanding, skills, and concepts. We know that every student learns differently and brings varied levels of competence and skill to the classroom. This observation is particularly applicable to millennials, who have a strong preference for learning activities that include options for choice and for setting their own paths to learning.

There is an alternative—teaching a la carte! In this approach to course design (Thompson and Grabau 2004):

- individual differences are acknowledged;
- the demonstration of learning can occur in a variety of ways;
- and students are provided with an opportunity to select their own learning activities from a menu of choices.

The implementation of teaching a la carte requires three easy steps:

Step One: Identify those basic learning activities and course requirements that you believe all students should complete. Examples might include reading the assigned text, class attendance, engagement in classroom discussions, or participation in tests, quizzes, and examinations.

Step Two: Create a "menu" of additional learning activities that students can choose from as a way of demonstrating their learning and their ability to apply the information that they are gaining through their reading and participation in class. A sample menu is included.

SAMPLE MENU

The following is a list of potential items that could be included in a learning menu (along with some ideas regarding point values based upon a 1,000-point scale). Each of these items have been field tested. The reader will need to judge the relevance of these activities to his or her own discipline or the degree to which they should be modified.

Interviews of Professionals in the Field (200 points)

Interview a minimum of three professionals currently employed in the human services field (e.g., teacher, social worker, psychologist, probation officer). Prepare a summary of your interviews, synthesizing the data obtained and generating relevant conclusions and observations.

Research Paper (200 points)

Write a research paper on one of the following topics (or one that is pre-approved by the instructor). Your research paper should be five or more pages in length (word processed, 12 pt. font, double spaced, 1-inch margin on top, bottom, and sides). Include a reference page citing a minimum of six references from professional literature (with emphasis on articles appearing in refereed journals). A rubric will be provided to specify guidelines and grading expectations.

Video Reviews (200 points possible)

Watch 8 videos/DVDs that relate to the topic/content of this course. Provide a written review of each video/DVD using the approved format.

Read and Write (200 points)

Choose a book from the list provided by your instructor. Write a three-page essay containing the following components: (1) basic thesis of the book; (2) a section of the book that had the greatest

---

impact on you as a person; (3) spiritual applications and connections to your faith in God; and (4) implications of this book for you as a human service professional.

Shadow a Professional in the Field (200 points possible)

Shadow a professional in the area or field of human services that you are considering as a focus for your vocation/calling. Journal your experiences and those insights.

Develop a Resource Notebook (150 points)

Develop a resource notebook of materials that will be useful to you. The resource notebook should be a minimum of 100 pages of content selected from a variety of sources. Organize these resources with topical dividers.

Share a Motivational Comment with the Class (150 points)

As a means of integrating your faith with your new knowledge and information, prepare a devotional for presentation to the class. The devotional should be 5–7 minutes in length and may take the form of a story, illustration, interpretive reading, song, dramatic presentation, etc. Make a connection between special education, the content of your devotional, and a biblical principle (including a verse or verses). A rubric will be provided. This assignment can be completed individually or in a group of two or three.

Create a PowerPoint Presentation (150 points)

Take some aspect of course content and develop a PowerPoint presentation that illustrates an important principle or concept. The presentation can only include a maximum of 10 pictures and 25 words. Be creative.

Provide Volunteer Experiences (150 points)

Provide 15 hours of volunteer services related to course content. Maintain a journal describing the nature of your volunteer services and the things that you are experiencing and learning.

Design Your Own Project (To be determined)

Submit a written description that includes the following components: (1) a summary of project activities; (2) the estimated time expenditure; and (3) the method/process for sharing results.

Step Three: Assign point values to the various required and optional experiences that will comprise your assessment system. For example, based upon a 1,000 point system, students would be presented with the following alternatives:

- Readings in textbook   100 points (required)
- Class attendance   100 points (required)
- Quizzes   100 points (required)
- Mid-Term Examination   100 points (required)
- Final Examination   100 points (required)
- Choices from the "menu"   500 points (of the students' choosing)

Under this proposed arrangement, students can select any combination of activities that total 1,000 points (or more if they so choose). At the end of the semester, the total number of points that students accrue (from required and selected items) will determine their final grade in the course. Students are in control of their own destinies.

Going a Step Beyond A La Carte

The a la carte process provides a structure of student choice within a specified set of parameters (i.e., point values and acceptable choices). This process may, when appropriate to the courses of study and the degree program, be taken a step further by facilitating a discussion on the actual development of the course syllabus.

SOME CLOSING THOUGHTS

A delicate balance exists between pursuing the learning outcomes for a course or workshop, and remaining open along the way to change the planned methodologies in favor of a strategy developed in collaboration with students. This paradox is, in many ways, the essence of teaching adult learners. We demonstrate our acceptance of the learner as a partner and fellow traveler on the path to understanding by remaining open to the possibility that we don't know all the answers. Perhaps we haven't considered all the pedagogical possibilities. Nor can we predict all the things that will emerge and occur in the learning environment. Thus, we refrain from rejecting other possibilities for accomplishing the task of learning in more effective, unpredictable, and possibly intriguing ways.

In the final analysis, the learning outcomes should ultimately drive the decision-making process. The successful teacher will always keep one eye on the destination—the place where we want students to be in their learning at the end of the process. In twenty-first-century terms, we begin the trip by punching the final location into our Global Positioning System (GPS). Along the way, if we encounter traffic jams, auto accidents, or construction zones, the all-knowing GPS chooses an alternate path that gets us to where we want to go. In the classroom, the teacher must become the GPS. Part of this responsibility involves an awareness of the environmental factors that wisely lead to alternate paths. Involve your students in this process.

4
VALUE MY EXPERIENCE

Experience is not what happens to a man; it is what a man does with what happens to him.

— Aldous Huxley

Think for a moment about some of the great stories you've heard over the course of your lifetime. These stories may be recalled from a variety of sources. You might remember the bedtime stories of childhood, books you've read, storylines of a favorite movie, legendary historical events, postings on an internet blog, or personal accounts that were shared by a friend. As these stories are told, read, heard, or seen, they carry with them a great potential for impacting us in a variety of ways. Coles, a Harvard psychiatrist and author, describes this phenomenon and potential as the "call" of stories (1989). Witherell and Noddings (1991) describe the power of stories and narrative as follows:

> Stories and narrative, whether personal or fictional, provide meaning and belonging to our lives. They attach us to others and to our own histories by providing a tapestry rich with threads of time, place, character, and even advice on what we might do with our lives. The story

fabric offers us images, myths, and metaphors that are morally resonant and contribute both to our knowing and our being known (Witherell and Noddings 1991, 1).

Stories and narratives, regardless of their source or format, provide a wonderful way for teachers to connect with students in the classroom. A challenging concept or complex principle can often be illustrated or emphasized through the power of a story. As we watch the characters of a story wrestle with their own values, engage the challenge of relationships, or weigh the alternatives they might pursue in response to a life decision, we sometimes find ourselves unconsciously and involuntarily drawn into the tensions of the story. Then we make connections between those life events and our own personal experiences.

Consider for a moment the rich histories sitting in your classroom—your adult learners. When thinking about adult learners and their unique contributions to the learning environment, remember that:

> Adults have a greater depth, breadth, and variation in life quality of previous life experiences than younger people . . . Past educational or work experiences may color or bias the . . . perceptions about how education will occur. If successfully guided . . . former experiences can assist the adult to connect the current learning experiences to something learned in the past. This may facilitate in making the learning experience more meaningful. However, past experiences may actually make the task harder if these biases are not recognized as being present by the teacher (Russell 2006, 369).

The challenge for the great teacher is to find ways to engage students in a rich dialogue that brings forth experiences and connects them with the topic of discussion. Vella (1994) would propose that making those connections is the responsibility of the learner. Conversely, what the effective teacher does is to provide a classroom culture that invites students to make those connections, even if it means making mistakes, engaging in spirited disagreements, or feeling foolish or confused—all on the way to understanding. It's the journey that makes the destination a valued place at which to arrive.

TOOLS OF THE TRADE

The Power of Narratives for Adult Learners

Each of us carries a variety of intriguing and unique personal narratives: the stories of our lives. This reality applies equally to faculty and students. Our individual narratives are in a constant state of development and refinement and as we have new experiences, alter our perspectives, examine and modify our personal goals, and learn along the way as we build and maintain relationships with the variety of people who enter our lives.

As adult learners arrive, they also bring along their personal narratives. The ways they view the ideas, concepts, and key principles of the courses we teach are translated through the lenses that comprise their own narratives. This reality provides a wonderful opportunity for learning. Through structured learning experiences, discussions, and reflection, students are provided with a means for assessing their own narratives in light of the lessons learned from the experiences, challenges, and insights of others.

As a final thought, don't underestimate the power of your own story as a significant teaching tool. Students are quickly drawn into the story that surrounds the passion that you hold for your discipline, and how that passion has impacted the path of your life. Consider the following ways of including narratives in the instructional process.

Fictional Literature

There is an abundance of amazing narratives that can be found in fictional literature. For virtually every academic discipline, there are a number of books, short stories, and poems that can teach important principles. The dilemmas, moral challenges, and difficult decisions faced by fictional characters provide a rich landscape for classroom discussion. As an example, consider the book *Speed of Dark* by Moon (2005). This book is the story of Lou Arrendale, a young man with autism. The reader is invited into Lou's world and becomes acquainted with the joys and challenges of his life, the nature of his relationships, and his strategies for addressing the routines and surprises of daily life. Lou, and the other people with autism who work with him, are invited to participate in a medical cure that would allow them to become normal. This story has possible connections and implications in the fields of education, science, economics, philosophy, theology, and political science (just to name a few).

In one class that read this book during a recent semester, the students could not wait to discuss what they were learning and observing from the story. Some students even admitted to extracurricular diversions as they read parts of the book that extended beyond the class assignment. How often have you observed that happening? It's pretty exciting!

History

History is often a study of the headlines that surround the great events of the past—dates, times, key historical events, and characters. As we all know, however, there are a number of personal interest stories and narratives behind those headlines. Consider using journals, personal letters, and other first person sources to illuminate the people behind history and the types of challenges they faced in making difficult life decisions.

Music

Song lyrics are a rich source of narrative. Music has often been used as a venue for social change. Consider using the lyrics of current songs that your students are familiar with as sources for political and cultural discussions.

Internet Sources

Many of our students, sometimes referred to as "digital natives," have been raised in a technological environment. They may be actively involved in social relationships through a variety of electronic venues: Facebook, MySpace, and blogs. This concept can be used to great instructional advantage:

- Create a blog for your class at one of the many free Internet blog sites (e.g., www.blogger.com).
- Use Blackboard (or other electronic classroom management systems) to post discussions on varied course topics.
- Ask your students to communicate with you via e-mails regarding specific course topics and how they intersect with their lives.

Films and Television

New films appear in theaters every week. Popular television programs that carry a strong narrative are often a topic of conversation among our students. Capitalize on these strong cultural influences by assigning students to critically review and analyze current movies. Ask them to comment on the film's narratives, their connection with your course content, and how those narratives intersect with their own lives and narratives. Think of this process as three sides of a triangle: (1) the narrative of the movie, (2) the connection between the narrative and the discipline, and (3) the connection between the narrative of the story and the narrative of their own lives.

SOME CLOSING THOUGHTS

By the nature of their positions, teachers own specialized knowledge related to the subject matter upon which the class or seminar is focused; that should be a given. However, two other factors are equally as important for teachers: (1) the realization that students sitting in the classroom have a vast amount of experience and practical knowledge that will greatly enhance the quality of what occurs in the classroom or learning environment; and (2) a willingness to partner with students, and to demonstrate a belief in the value of their experiences and knowledge by providing opportunities for them to share, discuss, and contribute in a variety of ways. Capitalize on both of these learning assets, and your teaching will never be the same.

5
CONNECT MY LEARNING AND MY LIFE

You can't teach people everything they need to know. The best you can do is position them where they can find what they need to know when they need to know it.

—Seymour Papert

Think back for a moment to our original discussions about the nature and needs of adult learners. The National Center for Educational Statistics described adult learners as people who have delayed their learning experiences because of other life demands, who participate in the learning environment on a part-time basis for at least part of the academic year, and who are employed thirty-five hours or more per week. They can also be financially independent, have dependents other than a spouse, may often be a single parent, and sometimes do not hold a high school diploma. These are people with a mission! In spite of the varied demands of their lives, they spend their time and financial resources to accomplish a personal goal related to learning. In many ways, their needs are practical and immediate.

Additionally, the psychological orientation of adult learners represents a sense of purpose and urgency. The adult learner has made a conscious choice to put aside or reduce the role of some aspects of life (e.g., free time, home and family responsibilities, finances, relationships) to seek the delayed gratification that comes from pursuing coursework or a degree. Parker Palmer (1999) describes this sense of focus and urgency, using his characterization of vocation, as follows:

> Today I understand vocation . . . not as a goal to be achieved but as a gift to be received. Discovering vocation does not mean scrambling toward some prize just beyond my reach, but accepting the treasure of true self I already possess. Vocation, at its deepest level is . . . something I can't not do, for reasons I'm unable to explain to anyone else and don't fully understand myself, but that are nonetheless compelling (Palmer 1999, 10).

The wise teacher will capitalize on the here-and-now needs of adult learners. While these adults will accept the need to learn theoretical concepts, they possess an expectation that those theories can be tied to usable, real-life information that is directly applicable to their current or future life situation (e.g., vocation/career, current job requirements, improvement of life circumstances, perspectives on current situations). As we will demonstrate, this can be accomplished by adding intentional activities to the course curriculum and instruction.

TOOLS OF THE TRADE

A Change of Venue

There are times when it's necessary to provide an added impetus for the beginning of a discussion or dialogue. When this occurs, the teacher has a wonderful opportunity to infuse some excitement into the lesson by giving the students an unexpected assignment. For example, in a recent class, the students appeared to be tired, uninvolved, and disengaged. They were generally unwilling to participate in discussions and, when pressed, would give very short and shallow responses to the questions that were being posed by the teacher. It was one of those painful moments in teaching.

Then the students were placed into groups and given the assignment of creating a television commercial that illustrated the topic of discussion. New life and a renewed sense of energy filled the classroom.

In another class, where the teacher's dilemma was similar, students were asked to rearrange their chairs into rows similar to airplane seating (i.e., groups of two or three with an aisle down the middle). Students were assigned roles and randomly placed into the "airplane." The students were told that they had been randomly seated next to an individual for a two-hour airplane ride. Their assignment was to discuss the controversial topics of the day's lecture. Even though the topic and assignment had not changed, the change of seating and the simulated airplane scenario ignited a flurry of discussion and activity.

Give Me Five

There are times that we ask a question and get a quick and superficial response. One way to encourage students to dig deeper into the question is to challenge them to provide a specific number of additional responses to the question. At these times you would say, "That is a great answer! Let's think of five other reasons why . . . " (while holding up a hand with five fingers). Continue the process as the students provide responses by manually counting down to zero with your fingers.

Designated Hitter

In this activity, students are placed into groups and given a list of discussion questions. As they discuss each question or topic, they are also asked to identify the individual in their group who will synthesize and share their team's responses with the larger group. This creates an immediate means for gaining summaries of the discussions from each small group.

Picture This . . . or Sing It

As a way of capitalizing on the multiple intelligences in your classrooms, assign students to small groups and ask them to capture the major aspects of a concept or body of information in varied formats, such as a(n):

- Poster
- Rap, poem, or song
- Brief drama
- Television commercial
- News interview
- On-the-street interview
- Human sculpture
- Picture without words

You're a Poet and Don't Know It!

A great and often unexpected way of helping students to process and summarize newly acquired knowledge is to encourage them to write poems. One quick and easy type of poem that students typically enjoy is the cinquain. This is a five-line poem written in a number of formats. For example, one type of cinquain is written as follows:

- Line 1: A title of one word or one subject
- Line 2: Two words about the subject
- Line 3: Three verbs that signify action
- Line 4: Four words telling about your feelings for line one (words or phrase)
- Line 5: A synonym for line one

An example may be helpful. Consider the topic of pizza and the poem that emerges from our thoughts about this important topic:

- Pizza
- Cheesy, gooey
- Grab, chomp, savor
- Greasy pleasure and enjoyment
- Ecstasy

The writing of cinquains can provide a great change-of-pace classroom activity. At the end of a lecture or section of course content, break the class into small groups and assign each group one key word or concept from which to develop a cinquain poem. Have the groups work together and then share the results of their creative thinking.

Service Learning

The term "service learning" has become a common part of conversations in higher education. As such, it is a term that has taken on a variety of meanings. Rhoads and Howard (1998) call service learning "a pedagogy of action and reflection." Weigert (1998) identified six common themes that should be considered as criteria for a true service learning experience:

1. Students provide a meaningful service.
2. The service that students provide meets an identified need or goal.
3. Members of the community are actively involved in defining the need.
4. The services provided have a direct connection to the learning outcomes of the course.
5. There is an element of reflection by the student.

6. There is an explicit understanding that students are being evaluated on their reflections and learning . . . not on the fact that they have provided a service.

These criteria for service learning send several strong messages:

- The identified service meets a need beyond simply providing an assignment for students to complete. The need is one that is felt and defined by the recipients of the service (e.g., the community).
- Learning is an expectation of the process. Learning can include skill acquisition, application of knowledge and skills acquired in the classroom, and the development of dispositions related to serving others.
- It is critical that students reflect on what they are learning. One of the factors that separates service learning from community service is the intentional emphasis on reflection. In a service learning paradigm, students take stock of their service experience from a variety of perspectives.

Part of this discussion must be related to faculty members and their role in modeling service as a critically important part of life. Faculty may resort to playing the "I don't have enough time" card when asked to engage in service to the community or the world-at-large. There is no doubt that many faculty members have campus commitments and full schedules. The example of a faculty member who chooses to actively serve alongside his or her students can be compelling as well. This picture sends a powerful message and enhances the credibility of the need for all of us to assume the role of servants.

Mother Teresa was once asked how she had managed to accomplish such great things in her life. She responded, "None of us can do anything great on our own, but we can all do a small thing with great love." Faculty members who serve are models of this philosophy. This lesson is a far greater medium than any words they will ever speak in the classroom.

Making service a lifestyle is based upon several key suppositions:

- Service is always a choice. We can choose to serve or we can choose to look the other way. The choice is always there.
- Service is generally inconvenient. By definition, service is providing help or assistance to another person. Those needs do not always appear in accordance with our schedule (i.e. preferred time, or preferred way of spending time).
- Service is a way of spreading light and love. By making the choice to extend ourselves, even at the most inconvenient times or doing the things we find most abhorrent, we are shining the light of love and compassion into a world that needs that influence. Don't we want that for our students?

Do you have an interest in developing a service learning component into your classes and find yourself wondering how to get started? Here are some things to consider:

- Analyze course-related learning outcomes to determine possible connection points for the implementation of a service learning requirement.
- Make connections with people and agencies in the community who might have a need that corresponds to the content and focus of your course. This is the point at which your ability as a faculty member to effectively network with people in your community becomes an important asset on behalf of your students.

- Delineate your expectations for student participation in the service learning process (e.g., time commitments, behavioral expectations, documentation, formats for reflection, due dates).
- Maintain ongoing communication with service learning sites to monitor the quality of services that are being provided by students, and to troubleshoot any difficulties that may arise. When serving in the community, the work and service ethic, of ourselves and our students, sends a powerful message.
- Serve alongside your students as a means of relating more closely to their reflections and observations about the experience.
- Continually evaluate the process and outcomes to determine better and more effective ways of integrating this experience into the pedagogy of your classes.

SOME CLOSING THOUGHTS

A valued colleague recently shared a strategy that he uses in his classroom. At any point in the instructional process, students have been given permission to raise the question, "So what?"

This is not meant as an indication of disrespect, but rather as a checkpoint to assess the relevance of instructional content against the demands of the real world. Consider two possible responses to this question. If there is relevance and a connection to other parts of the curricular experience or future endeavors, then the teacher should be able to articulate those connections. On the other hand, if there isn't a connection, or the content doesn't really have any easily known relevance, then it would be reasonable to consider dropping that content from the curriculum. This analysis is not intended to be as casual or reactive as it may sound. It's only to suggest that effective teachers will critically review instructional content to determine what is important and what is, perhaps, irrelevant. Consider the option of offering your students the "So what?" option. Better yet, preempt their questions by analyzing course/lesson content with the "So what?" question in mind. This can be an eye-opening experience and a means to refine and sharpen what we teach.

6

I HAVE MY REASONS
FOR LEARNING

While . . . the case for lifelong education rests ultimately upon the nature and needs of human personality in such a way that no individual can rightly be regarded as outside its scope, the social reasons (i.e. democracy and responsibility) for fostering it are as powerful as the personal.

—Basil A. Yeaxlee

We live in a fast-paced hectic culture. This factor is particularly relevant for adult learners who choose to extend their level of activity by engaging in classroom learning. Arthur and Tait (2004) captured the blur that is often the life of adult learners:

> In today's world, for an increasing number of people, the division between their work and non-work lives is no longer bounded by clear time markers . . . Our research has confirmed that increasingly people study at home and at the place of work, during working times and/or in the evenings or at the weekends. Modern communications have severed the link between time and space. However, the downside of all of this is that traditional boundaries between work and home, work and leisure, study and leisure are broken down . . .
>
> The findings described here point to a number of highly motivated individuals who, despite excessively long working

hours and heavy workloads alongside demanding family commitments, are genuine lifelong learners, keen to develop themselves professionally and personally. We also found that while many employers were sympathetic and supportive to individual learning needs, their understanding of the time pressures employees had to bear while pursuing a course of study was slight (Arthur and Tait 2004, 233).

In response to this circumstance, and the identified needs of adult learners, efforts should be made to provide opportunities for reflection on what they are learning and how that learning connects with their reasons for pursuing additional knowledge, skills, and dispositions. Taking the time to reflect on the events in our lives is an activity that we often view as a luxury rather than a requirement. Our busy, fast-paced world has conditioned us to keep moving without taking time to reflect on where we have been, where we are going, and what we are learning along the way. A key component of learning is the process of reflection. Consider the following approaches to promote reflective practice (adapted from Cooper, n.d.).

The Mirror: Reflecting on Ourselves

In this type of reflection, we do an inventory of our own gifts, talents, strengths, and challenges. In relation to service learning, students may ask themselves such questions as: How well suited was I to this activity? What would I need to do to improve my performance? Did I fully invest in this activity? Could I have given more of myself? How will this learning impact my future choices in regard to serving others? How have I grown spiritually from this experience? How does this experience influence my beliefs about my life calling/purpose?

The Microscope: Reflecting on Ways That the Small Connects with the Large

In this part of the reflective process, students reflect on questions such as: How does this organization/agency/service fit into the larger scheme of things? Does this experience support and strengthen my ideas about the things I have been learning in this course? What have I learned about this community or this particular area of community need? Did I have an impact?

The Binoculars: Bringing the Large and Distant Closer

Questions might include: What does the future hold? How is this agency or service provider impacted by the political and fiscal climate? Who monitors the quality of services provided to this group of individuals? What can I do to support efforts in this area?

TOOLS OF THE TRADE

Focused Listing

This activity helps students determine what they can recall about a specific topic and clarify their understanding about key concepts and understanding. Focused listing is conducted in the following way:

1. Ask students to write a key word or concept at the top of a sheet of paper.
2. Within a set time limit, students are to write down (in collaboration with a partner) all of the related terms important to understanding the topic or concept.
3. Debrief the large group discussion by creating a master list as the discussion proceeds.
4. An extra process: categorize the group responses according to "Related," "Unrelated," or "Appropriate," "Inappropriate."

Picture This

This activity promotes reflective thinking in response to varied learning styles. By stimulating interest, critical thinking, and participation, students are encouraged to look at concepts from a different perspective (i.e., visually rather than linguistically). The steps for this activity are:

1. Ascertain which general principles, topics, or concepts will be illustrated.
2. Divide the class into small groups.
3. Assign each group a principle, topic, or concept to illustrate.
4. Each group creates its own illustration that symbolizes the concept.
5. Each group provides an explanation for its product.
6. Each group discusses and responds.

Alternatives to the Usual Research and Term Paper Assignments

Instead of the traditional research or term paper, students may write one of the following:

1. Article for a professional journal
2. Abstract for a professional journal
3. Book review for a professional journal
4. A simulated office memo, report, or briefing
5. A memorandum recommending action on a controversial topic
6. A letter to a public official or company officer
7. Letter to editor or op-ed piece
8. Update of text readings, stressing new ideas or research
9. Letter of critique to textbook authors
10. Think piece: comparing/contrasting, usual critical thinking skills

11. Microtheme: brief essay, two hundred words or less, in response to a narrowly focused theme
12. Biographical or historical sketch

SOME CLOSING THOUGHTS

Imagine that you just met someone new. As you engage in conversation and get to know one another, a rather disturbing trend begins to emerge. Every time a new topic of conversation emerges, and you attempt to interject a personal reference, story, piece of relevant information, or anecdote, your new acquaintance quickly moves on to another topic, or to his or her own perspective on the topic of conversation. In short, this process becomes rather tiresome and frustrating.

Take two. Now you are sitting in a classroom with other adults who come to the learning situation for their own unique reasons. As new topics are presented, the faculty member takes special care to invite students to share their unique perspectives, a relevant illustration, or an opinion. As students describe their approach to the topics of discussion, it becomes evident that there is a considerable amount of diversity (e.g., backgrounds, experiences, challenges, successes, life situations) in the room. The faculty member relishes this opportunity and promotes conversations that allow people to wrestle with their differences, expand their perspectives, and find new common ground.

These two anecdotes demonstrate vastly different approaches to interacting with adult learners. In one, the new friend couldn't care less about your experiences, preferences, or needs. She was the center of her own conversation and much preferred to share her own information and knowledge. The second story illustrates a faculty member who is in tune with the needs of adult learners and makes a concerted effort to engage the class in a positive and constructive way.

The research is clear. Adult learners respond most favorably to situations that invite them to share their unique contributions and reasons for learning. Find ways to connect with your students and take full advantage of the rich diversity that they can contribute to the learning process.

EPILOGUE

As you reflect on the concepts, theories, and strategies presented in this text, we would like to leave you with four basic thoughts to consider as you design and deliver instructional experiences to adult learners:

- Be fair
- Be fresh
- Provide food for thought
- Provide a foundation for far-reaching opportunities

BE FAIR

Fairness, of course, is a relative term and one that is often subject to personal perceptions. As we have shared from several perspectives, however, when working with adult learners, it's critically important to maintain ongoing conversations regarding assignments, expectations, and evaluation criteria. Secondarily, it's important for the faculty member to maintain an open mind in regard to the balance between what is really important learning for this course/learning experience and what I might be holding onto for unrelated or unimportant reasons. Learners are more astute than we know in observing the differences between these two decision-making paradigms. Be sensitive to the real reasons behind your instructional decisions and remain open to the distinct possibility that there may be a different way of looking at things.

BE FRESH

We live and work in a fast-paced culture. The information and skills that are critically important in your academic disciplines are changing and growing with great frequency. As a teacher, it is critically important that we are communicating the best and most recent facts and figures to our students. As learners, and even as novices in the field, your students will have a keen sense of knowing when you don't know (e.g., the answer to a question, a recent issue in the field, the most recent changes and future projections). Three maxims to consider: (1) stay abreast of current developments; (2) be aware of what you know and what you don't know; and (3) model your willingness and eagerness to be a lifelong learner by researching the questions that you can't answer.

PROVIDE FOOD FOR THOUGHT

The courses or workshops that you teach should have greater implications in the lives of your students than forty hours of seat time and the grade on a transcript. Your goal should be one of providing your students with questions (and answers) that are so intriguing that they occupy their hearts and minds well beyond the time they spend with you in the classroom.

PROVIDE A FOUNDATION FOR FAR-REACHING OPPORTUNITIES

At a minimum, you are providing foundational knowledge, skills, and dispositions that will serve your students' professional careers well beyond the time that they finish the requirements for their degree or certificate. To accomplish that goal, however, there are basic concepts and ideas they must master before moving on to more challenging tasks and responsibilities. One of the ways that effective teachers build a bridge between these two parts of the learning process is by continually giving learners a glimpse into what can be, what is possible, and an awareness of the questions that will remain long after the class time has ended.

One writer worked with a bright, young teacher who was always thinking about ways to expand the boundaries of what was known, and to create new and different ways of looking at old problems. That experience is both invigorating and challenging for someone who has been around for a while (and who may see some of the pitfalls that lie ahead or who may be somewhat fixed in patterns of behavior). As part of this working relationship, it was occasionally necessary to say, "The answer is that there is no answer." This phrase became a frustration for this young teacher and a challenge to find new ways to resolve the presented problem, even though many great minds that had gone before each of us had failed to find a workable, long-lasting solution to the problem at hand. The young, motivated teacher was never satisfied with that answer and took it as a challenge to find a way.

And he did—often.

Two lessons: (1) we can sometimes learn more from our new colleagues than from our old colleagues; and (2) there will always be new problems to wrestle with, and some will not have an immediate answer. As we learn from old information and the new colleagues that become our partners in learning, the possibilities for the future are endless and incredibly exciting. Learn from the old and from the new, and help your students acquire a vantage point that allows them to do both of these things well.

REFERENCES

American Association of Colleges and Universities. 2002. *Greater expectations: A new vision for learning as a nation goes to college.* Washington D.C.: American Association of Colleges and Universities.

American Psychological Association. *Learner-centered psychological principles: A framework for school redesign and reform.* http://www.apa.org/ed/lcp.html.

Apple, M. and K. Teitelbaum. 2001. John Dewey. In J. Palmer ed. *Fifty major thinkers on education: From Confucius to Dewey,* 177 82. New York: Routledge.

Appleby, Y. 2004. Researching adult learners' lives. *Literacy Today,* 38, 22.

Arthur, L. and A. Tait. 2004. Too little time to learn? Issues and challenges for those in work. *Studies in the Education of Adults,* 36(2), 222–34.

Ausabel, D. P. 1963. *The psychology of meaningful learning.* New York: Grune and Stratton.

Beaman, R. 1998. The unquiet . . . even loud, andragogy! Alternative assessments for adult learners. *Innovative Higher Education,* 23:47–59.

Bedi, A. 2004. An andragogical approach to teaching styles. *Education for Primary Care,* 93–108.

Bonk, C. 2004. The (not so) shifting views of human learning. Indiana University, Department of Education. http://www.indiana.edu/~bobweb/handout/learner.doc.

Brookfield, S. 1985. *Self-directed learning: From theory to practice (Jossey Bass Higher and Adult Education Series)*. New York: Jossey-Bass.

———. 1991. *Understanding and facilitating adult learning: A comprehensive analysis of principles and effective practices*. San Francisco: Jossey-Bass.

Buechner, F. 1993. *Wishful thinking: A seeker's ABC*. San Francisco: Harper.

Coles, R. 1989. *The call of stories*. Boston: Houghton-Mifflin.

Cooper, M. *Reflection: Getting learning out of serving*. (n.d.) Volunteer Action Center at Florida State University. http://www.fiu.edu/~time4chg/Library/reflect.html.

Cranton, P. 1992. *Working with adult learners*. Toronto: Wall and Emerson.

———. 1994. *Understanding and promoting transformative learning*. San Francisco: Jossey-Bass.

Davis, B. 2001. *Tools for teaching*. San Francisco: Jossey-Bass.

Freire, P. 1993. *Pedagogy of the oppressed (rev. ed.)*. New York: Continuum.

Garmston, R. J. and B. M. Wellman. 1999. *The adaptive school: A sourcebook for developing collaborative groups*. Norwood, Mass.: Christopher-Gordon Publishers.

———. 2002. *The adaptive school: Developing collaborative groups*. Norwood, Mass.: Christopher-Gordon Publishers.

Garner, J. B. 2007. *A brief guide for teaching millennial learners*. Marion, Ind.: Triangle Publishing.

Kallick, B. 2000. Assessment as learning. In P. Senge, N. Cambron-McBabe, T. Lucas, B. Smith, J. Dutton, and A. Kleiner eds. *Schools that learn*, 186–95. New York: Doubleday.

Knowles, M. S. 1970. *The modern practice of adult education: Andragogy versus pedagogy*. New York: Association Press.

———. 1984; 1998. *The adult learner: A neglected species* (3rd ed.). Houston: Gulf Publishing.

Knowles, M. S., E. F. Holton, and R. A. Swanson. 1998. *The adult learner: The definitive classic in adult education and human resource development* (6th ed.). Boston: Butterworth-Heinemann.

Kolb, D. A. and R. Fry. 1975. Towards an applied theory of experiential learning. In C. L. Cooper ed. *Theories of group processes*, 33–8. New York: John Wiley and Sons.

Littlefield, V. M. 1999. *My syllabus? It's fine. Why do you ask? Or the syllabus: A tool for improving teaching and learning.* Paper presented at the Society for the Improvement of Teaching and Learning, Calgary, Alberta Canada.

Merriam, S. B. 1993. Adult learning: Where have we come from? Where are we headed? In S. B. Mirriam ed. *New Directions for Adult and Continuing Education: An Update on Adult Learning*, 57, 4–14.

Merriam, S. B. 2001. Andragogy and self-directed learning: Pillars of adult learning theory. *New Directions for Adult and Continuing Education*, 89, 3–13.

Merriam, S. B., and R. Caffarella. 1999. *Learning in adulthood: A comprehensive guide* (2nd ed.). San Francisco: Jossey-Bass.

Mezirow, J. 1985. A critical theory of self-directed learning. In S. Brookfield ed. *Self-Directed learning: From theory to practice. New Directions for Continuing Education*, No. 25. San Francisco: Jossey-Bass.

———. 1991. *Transformative dimensions of adult learning.* San Francisco: Jossey-Bass.

Moon, K. 2005. *Speed of dark.* New York: Del Rey.

National Center for Educational Statistics. 2004. *National household education surveys of 2001: Participation in adult education and lifelong learning*: 2000–01. Washington D.C.: United States Department of Education.

Ogle, D. 1986. K-W-L: A teaching model that develops active reading of expository text. *The Reading Teacher*, 39:564–70.

Palmer, P. 1999. *Let your life speak: Listening for the voice of vocation.* San Francisco: Jossey-Bass.

Prensky, M. 2001. Digital natives, digital immigrants. *On the Horizon*, 9:1–6.

Rhoads, R. A. and J. P. F. Howard eds. 1998. Academic service learning: A pedagogy of action and reflection. *New Directions for Teaching and Learning*, No. 73. San Francisco: Jossey-Bass.

Russell, S. S. 2006. An overview of adult-learning processes. *Urologic Nursing*, 26:349–53.

Slattery, J. M. and J. F. Carlson. 2005. Preparing an effective syllabus. *College Teaching*, 53:159–64.

Slavin, R. E. 2006. *Educational psychology: Theory and practice* (8th Ed.). Boston: Pearson.

Smith, K. A., S. D. Sheppard, D. W. Johnson, and R. T. Johnson. 2005. Pedagogies of engagement: Classroom-based practices. *Journal of Engineering Education*, 94:87–101.

Terry, M. 2006. Self-directed learning by undereducated adults. *Educational Research Quarterly*, 29:28–38.

Thompson, J. A. and A. Grabau. 2004. A la carte grading: Providing students opportunities to determine their own paths to success. *Journal of Natural Resources and Life Sciences Education*, 33:92.

Tough, A. 1979. *The adult's learning projects: A fresh approach to theory and practice in adult learning* (2nd ed.). Toronto: Ontario Institute for Studies in Education.

Wikipedia. Orienteering. (n.d) Wikipedia web site. http://en.wikipedia.org/wiki/Orienteering.

Vella, J. 1994. *Learning to listen, learning to teach: The power of dialogue in educating adults*. New York: Jossey-Bass.

Vermette, P., C. Foote, C. Bird, D. Mesibov, S. Harris-Ewing, and C. Battaglia. 2001. Understanding constructivism(s): A primer for parents and school board members. *Education*, 122:87–93.

Walker, D. and L. Lambert. 1995. Learning and leading theory: A century in the making. In L. Lambert, D. Walker, D. Zimmerman, J. Cooper, M. Lambert, M. Gardner, and P. Slack. 1995. *The constructivist leader*, 1–27. New York: Teachers College Press.

Weigert, K. M. 1998. Academic service learning: Its meaning and relevance. *New Directions for Teaching and Learning*, 73:3–11.

Witherell, C. and N. Noddings. 1991. *Stories lives tell: Narrative and dialogue in education*. New York: Teachers College Press.

Wlodkowski, R. J. 2003. Creating motivating learning environments. In M. W. Galbraith ed. *Adult learning methods: A guide for effective instruction*. Melbourne, Fla.: Krieger.

ABOUT THE AUTHORS

CHERYL TOROK FLEMING, PH.D.

Assistant Dean for Teaching and Learning, Indiana Wesleyan University—College of Adult and Professional Studies
Cheryl received her BA from Indiana University, majoring in biology and secondary education, earned an MS from Indiana University in secondary education, and has elementary and secondary principal's licenses. She completed her Ph.D. at Andrews University in Berrien Springs, Michigan, with a cross-disciplinary major in leadership. During her career in K–12 public education, she taught science courses to middle school students, then served as a school administrator, in positions encompassing both elementary and secondary sites. Cheryl's experiences in education include inner city school settings, as well as small town and rural sites.

In addition to her work as Assistant Dean for Teaching and Learning for the College of Adult and Professional Studies at Indiana Wesleyan, Cheryl teaches for the Masters of Education, Transition to Teaching, and Business and Management programs, both online and onsite. Cheryl's research interests include cross-generational studies, faculty development processes, intercultural studies, first-year teacher experiences, and mentoring. She is the coauthor of *Viewpoints: Understanding the Issues that Shape Education Today* (Pearson, 2008).

J. BRADLEY GARNER, PH.D.

Assistant Dean for Teaching and Learning, Indiana Wesleyan University—College of Arts and Sciences

Prior to moving into higher education, Brad's career was focused on program and faculty development in K–12 public school settings where he worked as a classroom teacher, school psychologist, and administrator.

Brad is the coauthor of two books that focus on employment and people with disabilities. His first book, *Getting Employed, Staying Employed* was recognized and honored as a "Book of the Year" by the President's Committee on the Employment of People with Disabilities. He has also authored several journal articles and book chapters on a variety of topics related to teaching and learning. Additionally, he is the author of *A Brief Guide for Teaching Millennial Learners* (Triangle Publishing, 2007) and a coauthor of *Straight Talk: Clear Answers about Today's Christianity* (Triangle Publishing, 2004, 2008).

Knowing that one of the least discussed and most overlooked ingredients for success in the lives of college students is the quality of the teaching that they experience, Brad's greatest passion is assisting college faculty to find new and better ways to meet the learning needs of all learners.